My Little Book of Prayers

ILLUSTRATED BY
Suzy Spafford

Suzy's Zoo®

HARVEST HOUSE PUBLISHERS

EUGENE, OREGON

My Little Book of Prayers

Text Copyright © 2005 by Harvest House Publishers
Eugene, Oregon 97402

ISBN 0-7369-1495-1

Original artwork © Suzy Spafford. Suzy's Zoo® is a registered trademark of Suzy's Zoo, A California Corporation.

Design and production by Garborg Design Works, Minneapolis, Minnesota

Scriptures are quoted from the *International Children's Bible, New Century Version*, copyright © 1983, 1986, 1988 by Word Publishing, Dallas, Texas 75039. Used by permission.

Printed in China

05 06 07 08 09 10 11 / LP / 10 9 8 7 6 5 4 3 2 1

To:

_____

With Love:

_____

God bless Mommy and Daddy

Thank You, Lord, for my

©Suzy Spafford

and my sisters and brothers.
family. I love them so much!

A happy family
is but an
earlier heaven.

John Bowring

For mother-love and father-care,
For brothers strong and sisters fair,
For love at home and here each day,
For guidance lest we go astray,
Father in Heaven, we thank Thee.

Author Unknown

5

I have the best friends in the whole wide world. Please watch over them and protect them from harm. Thank You for my friends.

Friendship is one of the greatest joys in life.

Charles Spurgeon

There is a friend who
sticks closer than a brother.

The Book of Proverbs

Friends make life a lot more fun.

Charles Swindoll

There is a little garden path
(I play it is a street),
And you could never guess, I know,
When in it I a-walking go
How many folks I meet.

May Justus

Heavenly Father, please watch over me when I play outside. Keep me safe and close to home.

The Daisy

I'm a happy little thing,
Always coming with the spring;
In the meadows green I'm found,
Peeping just above the ground;
And my stalk is covered flat
With a white and yellow hat.
Little children, when you pass,
Lightly on the tender grass,
Skip about but do not tread
On my meek and lowly head;
For I'm the flower that comes to say
Winter-time has gone his way.

Scotch Folk Verse

Sometimes when I'm sad, please
always with me and that tomorrow

Be near me, Lord Jesus, I ask Thee to stay
Close by me forever, and love me, I pray;
Bless all the dear children in Thy tender care,
And fit us for heaven to live with Thee there.

John T. McFarland

There's a Friend for little children
Above the bright blue sky,
A Friend who never changes,
Whose love can never die.

Albert Midlane

help me to remember that You are
promises to be a better day.

Lord, thank You
peanut butter

for my yummy food—especially
and jelly sandwiches!

For health and food,
For love and friends,
For everything Thy goodness sends,
Father in heaven,
We thank Thee.

Ralph Waldo Emerson

Bless our food and drink, dear Lord,
and bless our little friends, too.
Help us day by day to show
our love and thanks to You. Amen.

Rachel Adams

Lord, help me not to be afraid especially at night. Gently remind

when I feel scared...
me You are never far away.

Sometimes the biggest act
of courage is a small one.

Lauren Raffo

Even if I walk through a very dark
valley, I will not be afraid because
you are with me. Your rod and
your walking stick comfort me.

The Book of Psalms

Dear God, sometimes I don't always feel like doing the right thing. Please help me to make good choices.

Heavenly Father, hear my prayer;
Keep me in Thy loving care.
Guard me through the coming day,
In my work and in my play.
Keep me pure and strong and true,
Help me, Lord, Thy will to do.

Author Unknown

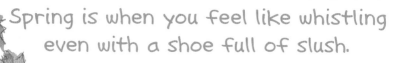

Spring is when you feel like whistling even with a shoe full of slush.

Doug Larson

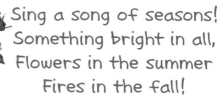

Sing a song of seasons!
Something bright in all,
Flowers in the summer
Fires in the fall!

Robert Louis Stevenson

Spring shows what
God can do with a
drab and dirty world.

Virgil A. Kraft

Thank You, Lord, for all the
flowers in spring,
the leaves in fall, and the

wonderful seasons—for the
the sunshine in summer,
snow in winter. I love them all!

When I look around my room, I Thank You for all my things,

Teddy bears are wonderful reminders for us to have soft edges, be full of love and trust, and always be ready for a hug.

Author Unknown

see all my wonderful toys and stuff.
especially my teddy bear.

When a child loves you for a long, long time, not just
to play with, but *really* loves you, then you become
real. Generally, by the time you are real, most of your
hair has been loved off, and you get loose in the
joints and very shabby. But these things don't matter
at all, because once you are real, you can't be ugly—
except to people who don't understand.

Margery Williams
The Velveteen Rabbit

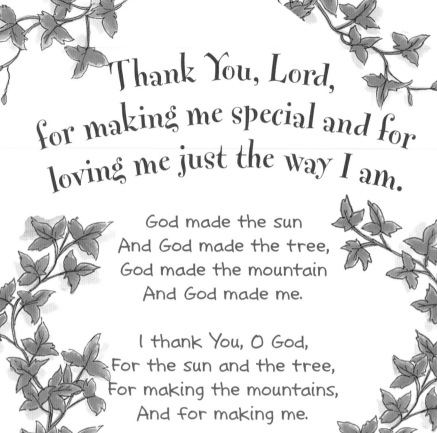

Thank You, Lord, for making me special and for loving me just the way I am.

God made the sun
And God made the tree,
God made the mountain
And God made me.

I thank You, O God,
For the sun and the tree,
For making the mountains,
And for making me.

Leah Gale

Jesus loves me! This I know,
For the Bible tells me so;
Little ones to Him belong;
They are weak, but He is strong.

Anna B. Warner

Lord, sometimes I see other kids

©Suzy Spafford

who don't have as much as I do.
Please help me to help others
with a grateful heart.

Savior, use the gift I lay
Humbly at Thy feet today;
May it bring some child to Thee,
There to live eternally.

Author Unknown

Father bless our school to-day,
Be in all we do and say.
Be in every song we sing.
Every prayer to Thee we bring.
May we in the lesson see
Something teaching us of Thee.

Author Unknown

Thank You, Lord, for my
Help me to be a good example

Be Thou with me every day,
In my work and in my play,
When I learn and when I pray;
Hear me, Holy Jesus.

Thomas B. Pollock

school and my classmates.
to them by having a great attitude.

Father, I want to always
and care for me. Thank You

Jesus, friend of little children, be a friend to me.
Take my hand and ever lead me close to Thee.
Help me grow in goodness, daily as I grow.
Thou hast been a little child and Thou dost know.

Author Unknown

Jesus, Friend of little children,
Be a Friend to me;
Take my hands and ever keep me
Close to Thee.
Amen.

remember how much You love
for the gift of Your Son, Jesus.

©Suzy Spafford

As I lay down to go to sleep, please hear my prayers and the prayers of others. Thank You for all the fun I had today.

Jesus, tender Shepherd, hear me;
Bless Thy little lamb tonight;
Through the darkness be Thou near me;
Keep me safe till morning light.

Author Unknown

©Suzy Spafford